For Val
Derek

For Steven & Jonathan
John

First published 1984 by
Walker Books Ltd,
17–19 Hanway House,
Hanway Place, London W1P 9DL

Text © 1984 Derek Hall
Illustrations © 1984 John Butler

First printed 1984
Printed and bound by L.E.G.O., Vicenza, Italy

British Library Cataloguing in Publication Data
Hall, Derek
Otter swims.—(Growing up; v.2)
I. Title   II. Butler, John   III. Series
823'.914[J]   PZ7

ISBN 0-7445-0132-6

Otter Swims

By Derek Hall

Illustrations by John Butler

WALKER BOOKS
LONDON

Otter's mother slides down a grassy bank and dives into the river. She does it again and again. But Otter only watches. He is frightened of the water.

This time she does not come back. Otter scrambles up the bank and stands on his hind legs to look for her. All he can see is a line of bubbles.

Is that her? Otter bobs up
and down anxiously, staring
hard at the water. Suddenly
he slips, loses his balance,
and topples head over paws
into the river.

Otter panics. He tries to run through the water back to the bank. He paddles his legs up and down very fast and cries. His mother swims towards him.

Now Otter is not so frightened. He swishes his tail from side to side like his mother. He's swimming! He twists and turns and glides through the water.

Otter feels excited. He takes a deep breath and dives down to explore. He sees fish flashing to and fro in the water and tries to catch one to eat.

When he gets out of the
water, Otter's soft, silky
fur is spiky and feels nasty.
But mother shows him how
to dry himself, as she rolls
and wriggles about in
the grass.

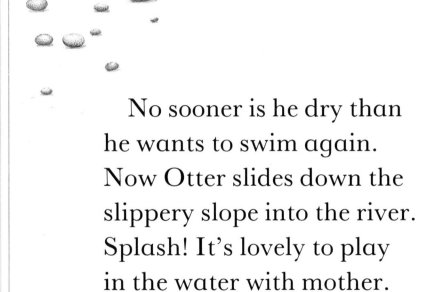

No sooner is he dry than
he wants to swim again.
Now Otter slides down the
slippery slope into the river.
Splash! It's lovely to play
in the water with mother.

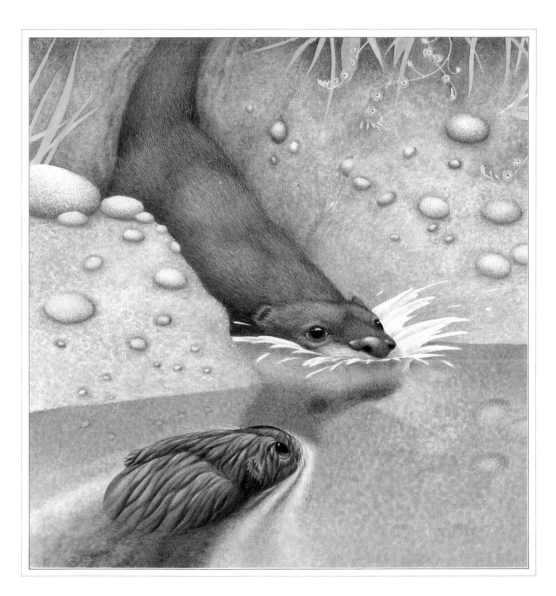